SMALL HOURS

*by the same author*

*poetry*
MONTEREY CYPRESS
THE COAST OF BOHEMIA
THE JUPITER COLLISIONS

*non-fiction*
ELIOT, AUDEN, LOWELL: Aspects of the Baudelairean Inheritance
SHAKESPEARE THE AESTHETE: An Exploration of Literary Theory
THE LIVES OF ELSA TRIOLET

# Small Hours LACHLAN MACKINNON

ff

*faber and faber*

First published in 2010
by Faber and Faber Ltd
Bloomsbury House
74–77 Great Russell Street
London WC1B 3DA

Typeset by Faber and Faber Ltd
Printed in England by T. J. International Ltd, Padstow, Cornwall

ACKNOWLEDGEMENTS

'Sappho to Her Pupils' first appeared in the *Times Literary Supplement*
and 'Edward Thomas' in *Branch-Lines: Edward Thomas and
Contemporary Poetry*, edited by Guy Cuthbertson and Lucy Newlyn.

A CIP record for this book
is available from the British Library

ISBN 978-0-571-25350-0

**FSC**
**Mixed Sources**
Product group from well-managed
forests and other controlled sources
Cert no. SGS-COC-2482
www.fsc.org
© 1996 Forest Stewardship Council

2  4  6  8  10  9  7  5  3  1

# Contents

I

## Pigeon

Any time I happen to open my front door
a pigeon batters out of the bay-tree opposite and stumbles
into flight as implausibly as a jumbo.

                                      At night, more
ominously, when the garden gate goes, it shambles
loudly off through the same shaken, protesting tree,
having slept, as it must, on its nerves. The bay-leaves
subside, and my own jumpy heart, before my key
goes home.

           The pigeon's world is no better than it believes
but I have sometimes known acts of kindness make me weep
for shame.

                Most nights, most people are not afraid to sleep.

# Canute

They'll get it all wrong – pretty quickly, here,
from what I learn of tavern-talk and gossip;
they say I told the sea that it must stop
inching up shingle to my throne's four legs.
That was my point. I did, and it did not.

Imagine setting up a throne on shingle
to prove the king's a man like other men,
the waste of time spent ordering the grey
dead waters to obey my windswept voice.
It was a flat grey light in which I sat,
the sea curdling a small way out, then running
free at its last breath up the sliding pebbles,
gasping and falling back but always rising,
rising until it splashed my sandalled feet
and I'd had it with telling it to stop,
shaking my sceptre, telling it again.

I got up, gathered in my robe and left.
The disappointed flatterers didn't follow,
not straight away. The servants brought the throne.
No, being king confers no special powers.
And yet one wonders. Yes, of course one wonders.

# Strewth

*EnergyAustralia, one of the country's largest electricity suppliers, says exercising the vocal cords in the bathroom adds an extra 9.08 minutes to a normal scrub. Singing, daydreaming, shaving and other 'non-essential activities' in the shower are adding to the average family's power bills and also contributing to global warming, it says.*
                    *– Daily Telegraph*, 23 October 2006

Song costs.
Time was it earned
a cut of mammoth,
paid for remembering
every deed of the tribe.

Then it was steak
lobbed by a king
for a long song
which lasted days
and bought that praise.

The cost of song
nowadays falls on everyman
as he sings, sings
and sluices in his shower.
It's too much. It has to stop.

But song considers
the lilies of the field.
Song wants to live
in the voices of unborn children. Song
may be the freest and the best of us.

## Sappho to Her Pupils

Live for the gifts the fragrant-breasted Muses
send, for the clear, the singing, lyre, my children.

Old age freezes my body, once so lithe,
rinses the darkness from my hair, now white.

My heart's heavy, my knees no longer keep me
up through the dance they used to prance like fawns in.

Oh, I grumble about it, but for what?
Nothing can stop a person's growing old.

Tithonus, as they tell, was swept away
in Dawn's passionate, rose-flushed arms to live

forever, but he lost his looks, his youth,
failing husband of an immortal bride.

*with acknowledgements to the translation by Martin West*

# Small Hours

Somebody has been reading
Book of the Week
but the radio's off. I've heard the gale-warning
for the sea south of us.

           Rain
runs caressingly down the outside walls
of every room.

           Yesterday, two printed
death-announcements arrested me, the first
for a man rich in honours
who had made a hundred and one,
the second, right above it,
for a child who 'fell asleep' on her first day.

The rain quickens and falters, quickens.
Grief gusts around us
in stories we shall never know.

To report on the dreadful
with an unflinching voice,
is that poetry?
           To say
life is terrible, man a morass
of contradictions?
           Or to move
like a person of leisure, of dreamed-of leisure,
from long curtained rooms
to the bright thriving garden?
           Ordered
as we would have it?
           Muse,

all you want is a few words
that will say how it was for us
at one a.m. on a Wednesday morning
so clearly that a thousand years may hear.

# Edward Thomas

We had lunch at his pub up in the wind.
It never blew. Amazingly
elderly bikers, silver-haired,
some of them leather-trousered, clogged
the car park.
              Much later, in the church,
in the visitors' book
below the memorial windows
(heart-shaking windows: Laurence Whistler)
I found a signature from only
nine years ago. Against it
'Artists' Rifles'. A man who might have known him.
Before that, though, we'd driven
a doubtful road until it vanished.
                      Rubble.
We parked and walked. We found the turning-point
and turned downhill.
            A slippery slope,
just enough roots across it
to stay, to balance.
           Underneath us,
almost vertically underneath us,
the valley, road and tiny houses
opened up like a gulp of distance.
               Beside the stone,
the memorial stone, a young couple lay,
lazing and sunning by the legend
cut in brass.
          We sat down breathless.

Born of a day in Lambeth. Died at Arras.

And I wondered whether that sad withdrawn man
would have laughed at this
almost unreachable memorial,
this knotty hillside dedicated to him
because he left here to seek the death
his poems ached for.

And I loved him, who had stopped wanting love
or anything. Who shouldered what he must.

# Midlands

I imagined
George Eliot country,
cattle stolid
in wet grass,
rivers that slowly broaden
past flat meadows
and fields of nodding
unripened corn
to the invisible sea.

I thought of close skies
darkened to monochrome,
of rain teeming
in streets of little market-towns
that turned to manufacturing.
Coal came and went
with the great age of textiles.
The Industrial Revolution
came and went like a high sea.

Its tidemark
is ripped earth, warehouses
ripe for conversion,
technology parks,
prefabs let
like lock-up garages,
call-centres, and industrial
museums welcoming
school parties.

The smoke has cleared.
TB and rickets
are back in cities, but these towns
are too small to support
such destitution. There are still
hiding-places, leaden pools
beside hunched willows
where a lonely child
might hear the creaking axle of the seasons.

Dark green leaves
and whiskery seed-heads
of tall fescue
climb the banks
of medieval ditches.
Stony paths and the sky
everywhere all day looking down.
Canals hidden
like avenues by trees

until the bank-holiday
holiday-makers come
in narrow-boats dolled up
like gypsy caravans
with new gloss
blue, orange, red.
Sluggish brown water
is briefly churned.
Splashing and laughter.

Going ashore
they seek provisions
from farm shops. Children buy
burdock-and-dandelion pop.
They heft cagoules and anoraks
in the unsteady weather
which, when it breaks, streams down
small windows full
of sodden foliage.

Morose afternoons
and sudden light at evening;
for perhaps half an hour
radiance from the west gilds
the flat land.
As summer deepens
and corn thickens
the new openness
widens the sky.

Splashing and laughter.
An observant child in the shadows.
A mind made here
would know how grimly
what lasts must grip
levels the wind
races across in winter,
trying doors,
clattering cans in yards.

# Jade

*i.m. Colin Davies, 1934–2006*

I remember you as a small man
walking the big fields,
shaking your stick
at dogs breaking from the bordering woods
when your dreadful Claire was on heat.

You were funny, contained, observant.
There was this boy
at the back of a lesson, glooming, abstracted.
You resented, you wrote,
his competitive gloom, and had

'told the good ladies at
[name of bookshop]'
he was to buy whatever he wanted
'in the way of a book' and put it
on your account.

The sticky tape is brown, brittle, breaks
as I unfold the letter
from long ago.
I remember suede shoes,
smells of spaniel and pipe-tobacco.

A First, a book, campness that hinted
at loucheness elsewhere, only
guessed at by us. You convinced
a bright historian
that the school had been given Hitler's leg-bones.

Good wine, but filthy cooking, I learnt years later.
I saw people scraping stuff into flowerbeds.
Waspish at times, unhappy
certainly, you painted landscapes
as a man at his true vocation. Two callings!

The book I bought is about jade.
I was entranced
by the stone's dull, impenetrable sheen,
its whites, its blues, its greens.
I was miserable and you were kind.

# Esmeralda's

*i.m. Mick Imlah, 1956–2009*

After I've read an email, forwarded,
I'm dozy, brooding over lines I wanted
to write about our birthplace, years ago.
*When Aberdeen was oil-rich, and the green-backed*
*sea paved with gold, with little scales of gold*
*that winked back at the unfamiliar sun*
*until it vanished in familiar cloud,*
*strange things were seen, and this was one of them:*

my mother tells me I've imagined it,
but I would swear the one time we drove past
the nursing-home where I was born, the place
had been transformed into a Mexican
with beer, tacos and late-night dancing. I'd swear
that this taverna was called Esmeralda's;
I see bright icing colours, pinks and blues,
and strings of gaudy lights made dull by day.

This afternoon, I'm gazing through the window
like a madman obsessed with counting raindrops
in the belief that if he counts them all
rain will suddenly rise up from the earth
in a wild skyward fling of glitter. Mick,
two months my junior, were we both born
under the one roof? Could be. Esmeralda's.
This is what the imagination does.

# In Memory of Keith Darvill

*1940–2008*

I

I could tell by the shelves of LPs
which house was yours; I didn't need the number
because their thin spines caught spare light
from the street; pale fishbone parallels.

You had said you were damned if at your age
you would become a morphine-addict.
You had a high pain-threshold
like my father.

At times your dark eyes
glittered, a trickster's,
and at times they were hazed
in reverie.

In the tipsy dawns
of the past, you had sometimes wept
at old songs ('Guantanamera'),
making conversation unnecessary.

Cooking, you were all clenched exuberance,
a pinch, a taste, a pinch, a taste
before you'd suddenly swoop the plates
down to your audience with your invariable 'Eat!'

II

Everything's now too late.
In all our arguments
I was poetry, you
were stage and radio

and a true teacher,
furious on behalf
of films I hadn't seen,
music I hadn't heard,

which didn't just mean Bird
but Smetana,
Pete Seeger,
Jewish celebration songs.

Thanks to our ages,
this was the only friendship
of its kind I shall ever make.
A joke along a bar

began it. Oh, the silences
men keep between them
when what they're keeping back
is what would spoil in being said.

# Two Occasional Poems

## 1  *i.m. Graeme Jameson (1940–2002)*

The giving and the giving and the giving
Are now a story that will not be gone,
Remembered for as long as we keep living
To pass it on to kids who'll pass it on.
Old friend, sleep softly. You have now become
A part of England and the life to come.

## 2  *For the Marriage of Anne Jameson and Julian Havil (2005)*

Under a spreading plane-tree, leafage gives
A space where we can breathe despite the sun.
Under the spreading of your love, our lives
Are freshened. May the two of you be one
Long years to come: today, the love you share
Renews us like that breath-renewing air.

# Two Wedding Songs from *The Book of Songs*
*for Cai and Xin*

I

A riverbank,
A pair of doves:
A good man woos
The girl he loves.

Water swirls round
Sweet watercress:
She bodies forth
His happiness.

His longing grows,
He cannot rest,
Waking all night
Like one possessed.

It's time to harvest
The tender cress,
For the lute to praise
Her loveliness.

Feast all your friends
With tender cress:
O drums and bells,
Please her you bless.

II

Bright blossom on the peach tree,
And the bride is preparing for her wedding.

The peach tree bears its fruit,
And she will be the mother in her home.

The peach tree's rich green leaves
Shine, like the good luck the good house deserves.

# A Suffolk Sketchbook

*for Robert Wells*

Deep as forever,
the great field of stars
over the cottage garden.

\*

I saw two meteors.
I heard a hunting owl scream
and a frog croak.

\*

Mishandled, a foresail
shrivels and folds,
a shred of yellow balloon.

\*

Like Special Forces,
the crickets transmit their messages
in brief bursts.

\*

Derelict timbers, vast sky:
a boat lists, stove in
like a breakfast egg.

\*

I shall be here
when you are long gone,
when you and your kind are long gone.

*(the Hepworths at Snape Maltings)*

*

In plastic buckets,
tepidly watered,
crabs crawled across crawling crabs.

*

At Dunwich,
it is said you can still hear
the bells of eight drowned churches,

as the syllables
of Beccles enfold
*beata ecclesia.*

*

Sails slice the wide marshes
of susurrant reeds,
their boats invisible.

*

The last bathers,
white, small,
inhabit an imaginary painting.

A slanting pink light
fades from the sea,
tousling the shingle as it goes.

II

# The Book of Emma

## I

She was brilliant. I was highly able. I understood this without ever being told or hearing it. Such were the terms in which we judged one another in our first competitive sizings-up of those with whom we would live then there. We were reading English. At the end of our first year we had Mods. She borrowed my essays on Yeats to use for revision. She got a First. I got a Second. Two summers later we sat Schools. The positions were reversed.

The first time I met her I was taken by a friend. It was a coldish night. A high wall on the other side of the road concealed everything except the black pinpricked sky. I felt the infinite crowding in.

We arrived. My friend remembered something elsewhere. He scarcely tried to be credible. So there we were. I and Emma.

She was housed in a modern block. Her room seemed very small compared to my own. It was warm and I think comfortable. She had her legs up under her in the armchair where she sat. I sat in the opposite chair. We may have had coffee or wine or we may have had nothing. The latter would feel more true to how we were. Awkward and fencing conversation.

She had slightly wiry hazel hair that curled. Even in flat shoes she was a little taller than I. She wore skirts or dresses. I have no memory of her in trousers. She was not quite beautiful but utterly haunting. Too many people thought we should meet for us not to have done. I wonder whether they meant us to become lovers. I wondered then. We did not.

Often she had a faraway abstracted look. She had read. I did not know that night whether I liked her or not. I walked back to my own college considering it.

# II

She had been on the Venice course. It seemed that everybody
except the vast majority had been on the Venice course. It
still exists. Bright young people learn about art and form
significant friendships. A school friend of mine had been on
it. I was talking to him on one of the first mornings when a
girl on a bicycle stopped and spoke to him. It was fleeting.
We were not introduced. I fell in love. She had long dark hair
and big liquid eyes. I fell in love. Moonstruck. Mooncalf.
Later I learned that she was very close to Emma. Often one
saw them together. I had not met Emma at this point. Emma
was talked about as a person of extraordinary gifts. All of
them seemed to think of her as someone exceptional. A
nunnish ardent mind perhaps. Indeed she looked quite like
Anna Akhmatova as her lover painted her. Aloof and tall.
Half nun half whore Zhdanov screamed. Emma had lovers
but she was not promiscuous.

# III

I spent an hour today on the Internet to discover what footprints had been left by people I was educated with in England or America. The size of an Internet footprint means nothing about the value of a life. The operating system I use is Windows XP Service Pack 2. It has a shelf-life. At some point support will be withdrawn. Microsoft euthanase their older products. Two people I was educated with became employees of Microsoft. One was a very sharp black-haired child in Detroit. I remember his smile. I like to think I recognise it. He has retired. The other was English. He displays on his website alluring photos of mountains in the United States. He enjoys hiking. He once almost fell through a skylight. Our housemaster was incredulous. Both boys have been successful.

You never heard of the Internet Emma. You died before the Berlin Wall came down. We were children of the Cold War. Whether you were a Cold Warrior I do not know. I was faintly shocked when a senior colleague said to me he was a proud Cold Warrior. He had played a distinguished unsung part. We were at Oxford when the nuclear threat seemed marginal. Robert Lowell said at the Union that like all great fears it would return. I remember discussing with S how we would deal with one of our children should he or she develop the clear symptoms of radiation-sickness. We would by then be living under a door propped lengthways against a wall. We would be listening to the radio. This was when the cruise missiles of which you never heard came. We could imagine mercy-killing.

You have left no footprint on the Net. There is no point googling your name. We always knew at some level that an

eight-minute warning might be all we'd get. You had to have
known at least that. Whether it worked in our bones like
the radioactive isotope of strontium we were exposed to by
atmospheric testing in our childhood I don't know. Or in our
souls. Whether life seemed more gratuitous. Whether consid-
ering our children's deaths was a deep deep damage. Whether
it reflected one done already. When you were still alive.

# IV

Whom the gods love die young. I have seen this attributed to the Homeric Hymn to Apollo. To Herodotus. To Menander. To Plautus. It is a thought that feels more Greek than Roman in its cold acceptance that the bulk of the bulk of lives is not worth living. It is a commonplace of heroic times. Glory is won by memorable sayings and heroic deeds. Deeds are better than words. Heroic deeds are almost always performed by athletic young men. If glory is the greatest good it is most greatly gained by heroic death.

Several people whom we both knew grew up very fast after leaving Oxford. They launched careers and pursued advancement. They developed gravitas. They knew what promotions what gongs awaited them. Taking silk. Getting one's K. They seemed to die inwardly. Admirable useful functionary lives. R maybe drank himself to death because he could see that this was his destiny. Silk has been taken. The first knight has been dubbed.

But many will say these are not heroic times and that this is a good. I also. Spared war we have not had to learn the limits of our physical courage. In the First World War Hemingway came to Europe as an ambulance-driver. He never got over not having seen action. He went to bullfights. He shot animals. In the Second World War he moved ahead of the American lines. He almost certainly did see action. This broke the law governing journalists in war-zones and had to be covered up. He was still the first American into Paris. He liberated the bar of the Ritz. Years passed and he shot himself. He could not face the drudgery of death by cancer. He could not face the common fate.

# V

## Old Boys' News
*HN and AG*

The coolest
of us all
is dead.

I imagine
white hands
on a white sheet,

the dragging breath.
The drug-pale
hunched swagger

(one afternoon
after a bollocking,
'I could use

a saggeroot')
has strutted
its last stuff

and died young,
my age,
along with Tiger

('Between the sheets'
was how he
explained his nickname),

between
what sheets
if any?

Knowing the who,
the when,
it's the how and the where

fill the mind
as a wasp
can fill a room.

Cold. Cold
white hands
on a white sheet.

# VI

Much of my childhood looks red. The red tiles of the kitchen at Harrowby Road the red Mansion floor-polish that buffed them and the red brick of our old house in Kepstorn Road. The polish was kept in a cupboard under the sink. At some point there was also a jar of something dark viscous and foul smelling that I associate with whooping cough. I ate my first whole raw carrot beside that sink. I had read that it would do me good.

Yet the breakfast-room at Harrowby Road was blue and the carpet in the drawing-room gold. Gold too was the fireguard in front of the two-or-three-bar electric heater in my room. I remember Granny and I carrying it between us from Kepstorn Road the hundred-and-fifty or so yards to the new house. One night I upset some water and soaked my handkerchief. I spread it on the guard to dry. Fortunately one of my parents smelt the smouldering.

There was also the night I fused all the electricity in my uncle's house in Putney. We would drive down from Leeds after Christmas each year to stay with uncle aunt and cousins and I would ache for Harrods' book department. I still remember the old A1. It was a two-lane road that dawdled through small villages and high trees. I stuck a hairpin into a socket to see what would happen. There was a bright blue flash and my hand shot back. I must have had rubber-soled slippers. The whole house was dark and I could hear voices below.

Much more recently I had cellulitis and septicaemia. I became deluded. W somehow brought me raving back from Paris. On the morning of the second day in hospital the consultant came into my room and said he thought we had saved the leg. I was still too woozy after delirium to understand that he meant it.

In early January 1965 my mother made a pair of white elastic garters. They were to keep up the long socks I wore with my school uniform shorts. We had come back to England the previous summer from a year in Detroit. I was to test the garters by walking down the hill and crossing over then walking up the hill and crossing back to the gate of our rented half of an Elizabethan cottage. I remember holding the garters.

The older of my two younger brothers saw from the window of our bedroom what happened. Two cars came down too fast from the top of the hill. I was waiting to cross back. I saw the first car but not the second. Men from Cottee's garage at the bottom of the hill came running and carried me into the house. My brother A was alone upstairs and forgotten. It was many years before he could speak of it. I was placed on the sofa with a rug over me. My mother left the room briefly. When she came back the rug had fallen over my face. She thought I had died.

In the ambulance my face was black and the whites of my eyes were red. I was unconscious for four or five days in Colchester. One more day and they would have moved me to Cambridge for brain surgery. My skull was fractured. I have scars across both eyelids. I am slightly deaf in one ear. There is a tiny inexplicable and invisible bald patch on one side of my scalp. I announced my return to consciousness by calling the nurse a great hairy ape. My memory cuts out just before leaving the house.

As a teacher I would usually ask classes how many of them had suffered illnesses or accidents that would have killed them a hundred years ago. We often disposed of half the room. Always of me. I have been lent time.

# VII

When I was very little my mother would take me to see the pigs. I had red and white leather reins. I could just scramble up a dry stone wall to look over. Pigs and piglets grunted and budged and looked as if they were enjoying their mud and mash. I specially liked the piglets. They trotted or scampered round the recumbent forms of the sows. On other walks I learnt what the word cul-de-sac meant and sometimes made my mother come up and around these key-hole shaped roads with room to turn at the end among new houses with big windows. New houses of a new prosperity. The war was fading from view. My parents had lived through it but didn't often talk about it. My mother sheltered under the piano when Aberdeen was bombed. As I grew older I discovered how rarely any who had been through it wanted to say much. There were still bombsites as there were cobbled streets and late editions on Saturdays of local papers with the football results. There were still unshaven little men in cloth caps who had never eaten properly. There was a chain-shop called MacFisheries that I loved for the gleam and freshness of the fish and the ice. There were tiny biscuits with little twists of icing on them that I called mosques. There were onions in mince dishes until I said I hated them. Long slimy things that tried to bind my tongue.

# VIII

My mother had a gold bracelet. Its outer edge was lightly
scalloped. It was hollow and there was a tiny hole in it. One
day on a beach in Yorkshire a grain of sand passed into it
and it developed a rattle I always heard when my mother
moved about. It was one of the defining sounds of my child-
hood. Another was her playing the piano in the evening. She
played mainly Beethoven Chopin and Liszt. Old yellow
Czerny scores Granny had given her. After my father's death
she moved to a flat. None of us had room for a Bechstein
boudoir grand so it was sold. The sand fell out of the bracelet
after some years.

# IX

Your girlhood is invisible to me. I find myself rereading your father's obituary. He died this year at eighty-three. His life is on line. He is praised for his work in conservation. He saved the island of Lundy from dereliction. He was an oarsman in his youth. He was born into a banking family and became a banker. He was briefly a Member of Parliament. He was appointed a Lord Lieutenant. He resigned because he found it tedious. A knight and a Companion of Honour. Financier landowner philanthropist. He had two sons and three daughters. I only ever knew of one brother and one sister. One daughter is said to have predeceased him. Predeceased. Like some weird elementary particle you flicker in and out of being. You are given and you are taken away. You are not named. Emma.

# X

We were so young. That now seems the extraordinary thing.
A year or so after you left Oxford and we largely lost touch I
was walking with AB past the Bodleian. I had met her at the
moment I met S to whom I was now married. It was a bright
spring day. We had been in the King's Arms and were making
our ways to different appointments. We were talking about
Foucault. I suppose that at that time Foucault would have
had the highest citation-index in Oxford theses of any living
thinker. We were not talking about sexuality or the circu-
lation of power. We were discussing epistemic shift. This is
what happens when a universally shared world-view is
replaced by another. Such world-views are often tacit. They
consist of agreements about the nature of reality. They may
matter most when they deal with what we think human
beings are. Althusser called them ideologies. There was a
slight blustery wind. We were excited by the novelty of the
ideas we were discussing. I was emphasising that in Foucault
history lacked a motor. He could not explain epistemic
change only describe its effects. Marx at least accounted for
change. Whether such world-views exist I partly doubted
then and am sceptical about now. Alexandre Koyré directs us
to the first known map showing the universe as infinite. It
was made by an Englishman called Thomas Digges in 1576.
It looks as if what philosophers of science call a paradigm-
shift simply happened too early within one mind. AB has
lived in Prague for many years now. She never expected that.
It is bewildering where the winds have blown us.

## XI

Reading his father's
obituary brings
Rupert Birley
squarely to mind,

the height,
the Londonderry profile,
eyes I remember
as slightly hooded,

the cigarette-smoke
blue in spring light,
the languor.
The two of us

were Honorary Scholars
with closed Exhibitions;
he had to sit
Penal Collections,

having idled a term.
I had neither the nerve
nor the inclination.
He passed by like smoke.

He was lost
swimming off Africa.
This morning, he is more vivid
than many living.

# XII

I am sure you and Rupert knew each other. Your brother had been at school with him. I can only think of one occasion when I might have seen you in the same room. It was a very large drinks party. The room was dark and lit in pools at the corners. The woman who was standing with close friends in front of the fireplace became an internationally renowned politician in another country.

You predeceased him.

He predeceased her.

She was assassinated.

# XIII

K in a brown velvet dress listening attentively to Tippett string quartets in the Town Hall with its strutting nineteenth-century aldermanic arrogance. They had wrestling there. D used to go. He was deeply amused by the elderly women who stood on their chairs and screamed at one wrestler to maim or cripple the other. C who gave me a watermelon. Who did not smoke in the street. A who gave me my first book of Montale. M after whom I sighed hopelessly and ineffectually. Who sat on her bed stitching a laddered stocking while I drank tea and tried not to look at her bare legs. SC with whom I had tea often. Earnest and puckish. Perceptive. Shrewd. Tea. Walking up the Banbury Road to have tea. And of course in our third year S. These are all parts of my other lives. I don't think they interested you. You also had other lives and they didn't interest me although I was always interested when your name came up. As I hope you when mine.

## XIV

The most intelligent man of my generation was pointed out
to me at a garden party late in our time. He was in the mid-
distance standing under another tree talking and listening.
It was a hot afternoon shading into early evening. Welcome
shade. I read a learned book he wrote later and admired it.
We have never met. I know the arbiter of taste for my gener-
ation but not well. We did meet later. I think you knew him.
Some people were in black tie because they were variously
going on somewhere. People were describing jobs they would
soon be doing.

# XV

I could find out. I could make enquiries. Many of these people have Internet footprints. Most do not. I could do what DS did. He hired a private detective agency to track me down before he flew in from the States. Being asked on the phone whether I was the Lachlan Mackinnon who. It would be mad. I am not writing a history of our times. I am not stalking you.

## XVI

As a child I had invisible friends. Benny and Lord. I did once try to distinguish between them but they were inextricably linked. I wasn't sure if they were human or not.

# XVII

At my prep-school there was a gang. Sometimes when I reached the dayboys' boot room they were waiting for me. They liked to make me shout yarooh like Billy Bunter. I had an American accent which made me strange. I was away for a term after my accident. What I hated seeing in the morning was the remains of the boarders' porridge. Each day a different boy brought it out and poured it out for the chickens. A slopped great dollop. If I arrived early enough it would still be steaming. I thought it pure waste. I wanted some for myself. When I became a boarder I resented the idea of porridge going to chickens. Grey then frosted with sugar. I never took the advice that someone with my name should put salt on it. Or absurdly walk about. Then the locusts arrived. The school had rebuilt the science lab and asked my father to declare it open. The locusts lived in a metal box with a glass front and a light permanently on. They lay along twigs. Sometimes I saw them copulating. The male seemed to lower the tip of his back onto or into the tip of the back of the female. I didn't want to look too closely. I made friends with the chief of the gang. I think I became a Major. Then one morning he told me I had been demoted to camp cook. There was no reason. I resigned and created MASEF. Mackinnon's Armed Services' Expeditionary Force would take on C's Army. They didn't. With two followers I managed some scouting and espionage but they ran away when it came to a fight. There must have been at least thirty in the other group. I had a friend CH who could do all the voices of the television comedian Dick Emery. He joined the school after all gangs had melted away. After he left I devised a plan for some of us to steal a boat in West Mersea and sail to help the Americans in Vietnam.

# XVIII

The evening I met you I already knew about the novel. I had
been told not to mention it. It was understood that you kept
it under your bed. I do not know when you had started it.
You never spoke of it to me. People had faith in it. Greater
faith than perhaps you ever knew. Someone was doing some-
thing. Something real that would tell all about ourselves.
That might define us. It was thrilling to think of. Of you
taking it out only in solitude and adding a few words at a
time. Or vanishing for whole days to blaze away. Of you
watching us all and turning our dross into gold. People
believed you knew something the rest of us did not. That
you had a wisdom that would naturally express itself as
men and women whose words and actions would be so
like life as to become our lives. That you would tell us who
we were.

# XIX

I had better talk about Thomas Hardy. We must have talked about him but I don't remember. I was introduced to Hardy's poetry when I was thirteen. I adored it for the intricacy of detail and for the technical variety. I liked it so much that by the time I was fourteen I wanted to own the Collected. Its maroon cover exactly matched the school hymn-book. I imagined reading this devout atheist in Chapel. I couldn't afford the book so I looked round for a prize to win. The verse prize was next in the calendar. I wrote two poems. Jon Silkin gave me second prize and I had discovered what I wanted to do. Reading Hardy was also the best preparation for reading Auden.

Hardy fell in love with a girl in 1870. They married in 1874. Something went wrong within the marriage. They were utterly estranged when she died in 1912. Hardy came across albums of sketches she had made during their honeymoon. Overcome with grief he wrote the Poems of 1912–13 which are his greatest achievement. In them he talks to a ghost. Her name was Emma. Emma Lavinia Gifford. Your name was Emma Smith.

Nympholepsy means a frenzy for something unattainable.

After Robert Lowell's reading at the Union I spoke to him and he agreed to see me the next day. A year or so earlier my father had arranged for me to interview him at the University of Essex where they were both teaching. When I arrived at St Catherine's in the early afternoon Lowell was still sleeping in. I went to the college library. In the *New York Review of Books* I found Elizabeth Hardwick's essay on Hardy's women. I also reread some of George Meredith's Modern Love. It is an account in verse of marital failure. Elizabeth

Hardwick was Lowell's second wife. Having chatted to Lowell in his room I was to escort him and his third wife Lady Caroline Blackwood to Wadham. He was dining there.

Blackwood is the dolphin of Lowell's book *The Dolphin*. She was still startlingly beautiful. As we walked she kindly and sensitively fell a few paces behind. Lowell asked what I was reading. We talked about Hardy's poems. Something good on every page I enthused. On every tenth page was Lowell's view. He asked what I thought of Hardy's women.

## XX

There was a wood behind the house in Harrowby Road. A stone wall surrounded it and divided it from the lawn. There was a proper entrance and a half one created where some stones had fallen down. There were six or seven oaks and undergrowth. Nettles brambles and wild grass. I played there for hours. I preferred the end near the sandpit. It was less overgrown and scary. I was happy. One night there was a storm and a branch fell through our neighbours' greenhouse. Men were sent for the next day to fell some of the trees. I believe I can make out one of the stumps on Google Earth.

# XXI

When I joined Grade 2D everybody was already notionally paired off. We were seven years old. J sat beside me and was away one afternoon a week for Hebrew class. I went to V's house. He was Indian and his mother wore a sari. He had a tiger-skin rug in his room and he showed me the bullet-hole. His uncle had shot it. G went off me when I said his father was wrong about the speed of the cheetah. He was indeed wrong. We sat discontentedly in the back of the black station-wagon one of the cooks picked us up in each morning. Each cook and I suppose cleaner had a car provided in return for collecting us. There were also buses. The first lunch I had was chop suey. I had never heard of it. The girl I wanted to be paired with was black-haired SA.

In my dream I was running for President with her at my side. At each whistle-stop we emerged stark naked. It was John and Yoko more than five years early. The dream excited me but I didn't know why. The Beatles were about to arrive in America. I had never heard of them but as an English kid I was expected to have a favourite. From the cards that came with bubblegum I liked the look of Paul best.

A friend of my mother's advised her to watch out for a new folk-singer called Bob Dylan. He might be a star in the making.

Mr M taught science and showed me a cow's brain in a glass tank.

I had a crew-cut. Outside the barber my father took me to there was a machine that dispensed balls of bubblegum in variously coloured candy shells.

I had never seen a supermarket or automatic doors before.

# XXII

Robert Graves had the lyric poet's habit of falling in love. It seems he truly believed that each girl was a literal incarnation of his Muse. Poets have believed madder things. I forget who wrote of the sad sight of Mr Yeats trying to believe in fairies. But the erotic imagination often forms its template young. You did not do that for me. N had done it at school. Only now do I suddenly realise how like SA she was. Black hair. So perhaps it had formed much earlier.

In my last term I was Head Monitor of my house. This entitled me to a bedsit whose windows gave out over miles of Surrey woodland. My heart still quickens when we pass Farnham and the landscape begins to take on the contours of passion. I adore the bogusness. Raw hacienda-style fences. Restaurants that come and go. Godalming boutiques. It's as though nobody born in Surrey ever stayed there. All are incomers inventing spurious continuities. A Chinese restaurant in an eighteenth-century townhouse.

Probably mooning over N I was sitting one morning in my study when someone knocked the door. With the lordliness of my position I said Come in. A shrunken old lady entered and I jumped up. She wondered whether she could look at the view. Of course I said of course. This had been Robert Graves's study. She had been the matron's daughter. He had brought her flowers.

# XXIII

High-breasted is a word Hardy might daringly have used to describe one of his heroines. In coarser times I write it of you and think how Victorian it makes you sound. Hardy wanted to write explicitly about sex and wrote a furious essay about English prudishness. Cryptic though his inner life was I do not think he would have been gladdened by the emotionally flattening effect of our pornographised culture. Explicit for him was not what it is for me. High-breasted slim girl you were younger when we met than my daughters are. I rarely had sexual thoughts of you. All else aside it simply felt dis-respectful.

# XXIV

The owner of the house my parents rented in Detroit had packed most of his books away. There were some boxes of them under my bed in the front room. I was forbidden to touch them. I naturally peeked after bedtime and I found a book about whales. The informative passages were inter-spersed with some sort of story I couldn't fathom. I wonder if I am the only person ever to have read Moby-Dick for the cetology.

# XXV

My father had a ferocious temper when he was young but governed it so well that I never saw a glint of it. I have only seen one picture of him as a child. A rather sad-looking little boy. Shorts and jersey. My mother said that his family had never understood him. Yet they were able. His father was an advocate. The son in L. Mackinnon and Son. There is still a firm Mackinnons but none of the family went into it. My uncle was the last and he kept places open for my brothers and myself. None of us took one up. At dark moments I sometimes wonder whether the ironclad respectability of an Aberdeen advocate might have helped me. Grandfather held up his gold watch for me to listen to the loud tick. The last time I saw him the muscles under his chin kept working like a frog's.

Grandfather was the eldest. Doris was I believe the first woman professor in the University of London. She studied biology. Lilias was a concert pianist with a fine future. She went to America. She refused to join the musicians' union and was denied all bookings. Esther had just exhibited at the Scottish Royal Academy when she died young. A melancholy painting of a stranded half-derelict boat hung at the bottom of the stairs in Manningtree. Alan took an Oxford I believe degree in English before the First World War and a degree in science at the Sorbonne afterwards. He published a novel I have not read. He wound up as Principal of a Northern Irish teacher-training college and captain of the Northern Ireland bridge team. He took everywhere with him a tapestry he was working on and a budgie which flew round the room. His life was ravaged by compulsive gambling.

Fifty per cent of adult male Mackinnons died at Culloden but we lived in Cumberland House after the year in the States. After a brief time in a rented cottage.

## XXVI

Toto was some sort of great-relation of my father's. Toto's chair sat in a corner of one of those spaces which is neither room nor corridor. A point of intersection. Two doors an opening from the landing and a staircase to the top floor. It was made of a dark wood which had at the least been stained darker. Not creosote. Some fine soaking stain the wood inhaled. The seat part was like a stool. It broadened from the back to the front. The back part slotted into the stool and sloped backwards slightly. It broadened gently to perhaps half the width again as it rose. It had been decoratively carved. High up there was a hole which might have been a heart but I think was a flower. I would guess she was childless. I do not know who lovingly made it or had it made for her. Toto's chair has long disappeared. We come. We go. I do not know what if any trace she leaves on others still living. What footprint. The chair was so small that even in old age she can have been no bigger than a child.

# XXVII

A new moon high above the Cathedral as I walk southward home through the early dark of December. The cold wind behind me whips along a few notes from the folk-band playing in the High Street. Mainly from the cutting banjo. If I take up another instrument the banjo may well be it. Emma we didn't like the same music. My taste was for psychedelic rock and some of the remoter corners of what we call the twentieth-century classical tradition. I do not remember music playing in your rooms and I do not remember us ever talking about it. A vague flicker tells me though that we did once. It would have been somewhere in Port Meadow. I mentioned what I liked and you hadn't heard of it. Of course there were gender divisions. Essentially rock music was for boys. I had a mission-ary hopefulness but only S ever responded. To be fair AB also but she had done it for herself.

I imagine you were a pianist. A girl of your background could hardly have escaped the lessons I abandoned for the sake of the blues. I never knew of your having a piano but I imagine you playing stormily romantic music to yourself at times when nobody was about. There must have been such times. I imagine your whirl away from the piano when you heard somebody coming in. Echoes fading. A book picked up. Pulling yourself together with a noli me tangere concentration.

## XXVIII

To reach you I used a landline. Nobody had a mobile yet. I do not remember why I needed to reach you. Perhaps some go-between had asked me to or told me I should. This would be the third or fourth last conversation we ever had. A man answered. From the speed with which he passed the phone I deduced he and you were in bed. It was afternoon. I envied your leisure.

You told me once about the night you were burgled. In some house I do not know where. You slunk under the duvet and rang the police. You could hear sounds downstairs. The police took half an hour to arrive. Robbers or robber long gone. The fear of violation or sudden death.

# XXIX

In our third year I was sent out to another college to be taught for the Special Authors paper I had chosen. The woman who taught me was a rising star in the faculty. She was said to have been propositioned by the captain of another college's rugger XV when visiting one of her undergraduates. Rugger was a word still in use. We say rugby now. I am astonished how many of my friends have played or are passionate about the game. That I have twice as an adult been taken to Twickenham. Soccer is now almost entirely used by Americans. The nineteenth-century public-school words finally died.

I remember talking about the different rates at which people and places age. She seemed more urgently aware of the relation between poetry and life than my other tutors. Poetry and the ordinary lives we actually live. I struggled not to show the tongue-tiedness she must often have seen. Because of her I read Adrienne Rich. From the tutorial times she offered I picked one which meant I could not dine in Hall that evening. I enjoyed walking back in darkness and hearing the wind in the trees. A solitary pizza in a pub. A time in my life of wild almost objectless yearnings.

From my rooms at night I could hear the wind crying in Christ Church Meadow. Crying and crying over an empty land.

# XXX

In the garden of the beginning, where the tongue
we speak is still electric with its newness, gung-

ho with the possibility of saying truth,
we hadn't learnt what the poems have always sung

would stick it to us too. Beauty fades. The best die.
I was reading in my study when I was rung

to be gently told she had gone away from us.
It was a blue room. Blue walls. A blue light-shade hung

up in hope of the writing I was getting done.
In the garden of the beginning we were young.

Now we are not. Years have frosted my once brown hair.
I dread an over-crowded future, where among

all those people not one is found who knows your name
or my name. Lachlan. It is her name I have sung.

The wind cries. Often it has seemed to sing of her.
I remember you as you were when you were young.

# XXXI

A friend of mine became a housemaster. I was waiting for
him one evening in the hall where the polished oak honours
boards were hung. I suddenly realised that for a boy going
away to school at thirteen the end of the Second World War
was now more remote than the end of the First when I went
away.

The Second War marked the landscape of my later child-
hood when we lived in the country. Pillboxes crumbled in
woods or at the edges of fields. Agribiz has largely ploughed
them under since. I remember walking past one at the centre
of a field on a November afternoon. High Essex sky and a
cold wind. Frost in the air. I was walking just ahead of a
young master from my prep-school and a boy with whom he
had formed a close friendship. We were talking about how
we should behave if a war had happened and we were the
last people alive. We did not think of war as slugged out over
fields like this one. We imagined it as a brief incandescent
breath erasing everything. This was the Cold War.

A road home my mother often took cut directly across the
two metalled runways of a field American bombers had used.
This had been abandoned but there were half-a-dozen Ameri-
can bases within easy reach. I looked out for their planes.

At the east end of Manningtree there was a semi-derelict
yard protected by high mesh fences. In it there was a non-
descript small building like an elaborated almost windowless
hut. A tall aerial stood beside it. My father thought it was
some kind of light industrial plant. Years later it was opened
to the public. Below ground was the control room from
which most of East Anglia would have been governed after a
nuclear exchange. Analogue clocks and a mad fantasy half a
mile from our house.

# XXXII

We came across each other in a road neither of us had much occasion to use. I fell into step beside you. I remember bushes to your left and a sound of running water. I didn't yet know that the sound of running water accompanies all Wordsworth's most powerful experiences of his imagination. Then we stood at an angle to each other. There was more colour in your cheeks than usual. It was a fresh day but you were more animated more willing to disclose. The day before you had been at lunch with the Poet Laureate Sir John Betjeman. You did have some grand friends though I never thought of you as grand. Moneyed yes but not grand. What occupied you was his terror of death. He had talked about it frankly and at length and was not to be assuaged. You found it hard to grasp. You wanted to know what I thought about it. It was the only time I saw you fazed by an idea. The whole subject seemed far removed from us those bright minutes with your face alight and the stream burbling. I said whatever I thought. You went wherever you were going and I went my ways to whatever. Your face impassioned.

# XXXIII

S and I were driven down to Rodmell by D. We saw the outside of Monk's House then went to the field my distant cousin Virginia Woolf walked through on her way to drown herself in the River Ouse. She was then D's favourite writer. Her novels have always quickened a claustrophobia within me. It was not a fine day but it was not raining. The grass was dark. The river was narrower than I expected. I introduce that haughty tall woman not to compare you with her. Not exactly. But when I wondered what she was like I often thought of you. The mercurial sensitivity. The aloofness. The withheld. It was the day of the village fête. A barrel organ which boasted in bright circus colours of having travelled half Europe cranked out its music. Bits of it moved. There was a small crowd. There was a weird disparity I suspect she would have enjoyed. That you would have enjoyed. I think you were still alive.

# XXXIV

God bless Mummy God bless Daddy God bless A God bless J. God bless Granny and Grandfather. Thank you for a lovely day and look after me. Make me a good boy Amen. That was the prayer my father taught me to say at bedtime when I was a little boy. He didn't go to church much but he was a profound believer. I notice now that the prayer contains no word of sin or repentance. Wisely. We live them later.

Half the people I prayed for are dead. All the years I knew you I was out of faith. Now I believe in one God. I believe in the intercession of the saints. I have had God knows on one occasion reason more than enough to give thanks to St Jude. I cannot become a Roman Catholic because being divorced I should be excommunicate on arrival. Yet I believe in the Real Presence and in the teaching authority of the Pope. I do not believe that I am bound to accept teaching without questioning. Yet there are things I now believe without question.

I remember no conversation with you about religion. You gave no signs of piety. You were too intelligent though for the milk-and-water atheism which was so often the outcome of an Anglican upbringing and still is. Atheism is properly as tough a faith as any. If it is a faith and not a parasite on the specific faith it rejects. I often wonder whether a Hindu atheist sees things in the same way as a Christian atheist. What brought me back to faith was the irresoluble nature of the mind–body problem. Mind may simply be the expression of our organic chemistry. May be but it doesn't feel like that. The mind draws on increasing experience but does not itself age. My hair has gone grey without my leave. I found these contradictions best resolved in the Incarnation. I imagine you had an Anglican funeral. I imagine a country church.

# XXXV

I had not travelled much when you died. Scotland. The West
Country. The Netherlands. The United States. Since you died
Prague. I have come to know Paris better than I know London.
Brittany. Normandy. The South of France. The Mediterranean.
I have sailed on a yacht from Marseille to St Tropez and I have
steered the yacht into St Tropez. Hong Kong. China. I had
vertigo on the Great Wall. Japan. Ankara. Istanbul.

I don't know where your family holidays were spent. After
Oxford you seemed to drift. You applied for a job which
suggested sympathies far more to the left than I had expected.
The woman who got it now sits in the Cabinet. You may have
taken a course in law. I don't think you worked as such. I
know little of how you lived. There was after all family money.
You went to Antarctica.

The last astonished me. I feared what the effect of the blind-
ing white gazing into your soul might be. I feared that was
what you sought. Only now do I learn that your father claimed
to have visited every hut on that continent. With him or not it
was at least partly him you were following or exploring. Of
that I am now sure.

# XXXVI

I joined the queue for the mausoleum of Mao Zedong. It ran down from the north of Tienanmen Square along the west wall of the mausoleum then round and in. J and M had decided to see the so-called Winter Palace in Beihai Park but this was what I had promised myself. The queue was about quarter of a mile long it seemed and about eight abreast. I was on the right flank. The queue was observed by young men with security passes hanging round their necks. They looked like the Red Guards of the Cultural Revolution just over twenty years before. They were I suppose secret police not afraid of being seen. Suddenly there was a flurry. Shouting. From a row about ten in front of me two of the young men dragged out a middle-aged Japanese man. They threw him to the ground shouted a bit more and turned away. He picked himself up and left in a hurry for the southwest corner of the square. I shuffled to the middle of the queue and turned my white face down.

The tiny Chinese girl now on my left spoke. She was eighteen or nineteen. It'll be you next. I asked why. They want our cameras. Follow me. We went over to a booth and took receipts for our cameras. We resumed our places. The elderly man next to her was her father. They were provincials. He was on a short contract and in Beijing for the first time in his life. He was seeing the monuments. We entered the mausoleum. No dallying. We went to the right of the catafalque on which the late Chairman lay. Only the head was visible. The body was decently covered. It may have been a wax effigy. It may not. Rumour had it that corpse and effigy alternated. We came out of the back of the mausoleum into a parade of souvenir stalls. We went back to the booth and reclaimed our cameras. I told her to tell her father that his daughter spoke very good English. She giggled with embarrassment and spoke. He nodded and smiled. He shook my hand. I left for my hotel.

Above all in China I felt the age of the place. When Shakespeare was born China had two thousand years of continuous legal records. The streets of imperial Beijing are built on a scale to dwarf all persons. Even the pavements are highway-broad. Mao's mausoleum lies in magical defiance athwart the great north–south axis of the old imperial city. It is a fiat.

Back in England our medieval cathedral seemed at first sight uncouthly modern.

# XXXVII

The dead are often seen among us. Last night I saw my friend
K coming into the pub. People shifted and it was an old
woman stooped as he used to be with his leather bag over
one shoulder and bags of new books and CDs in his other
hand. In the trick of a gesture or a shade of hair we see what
is impossible. We buried K less than a fortnight ago. I am not
thinking of such intimations as I think Emma of you. Yes I
have thought I have seen you. Never closer than in the mid-
dle distance nor for many years now. When I think I see you
now I know at once it is only resemblance to a girl long dead.
But at times the barrier between the living and the dead
seems to be merely a membrane of immense strength. We
push and push against it and sometimes the muscles of the
mind feel they feel an answering pressure.

# XXXVIII

At Ryoanji the fifteen mossy boulders are laid out on their islands of grass in a tray of raked gravel which looks about the same size as a tennis-court. You sit on benches along one side but from wherever you view it there is always one rock you cannot see. It is deftly turned and to my mind terrifying. There are brick walls with eaves and trees that hang a little way over them. It is the most famous of the Zen gardens of Japan. Going there you know already that it is one of the great holy places of the earth. There is an air of hushed reverence you cannot wish to break. But what it articulates is the profoundest void in which names have no meaning all desires are forgotten and unreality is accepted as the underlying condition of our being. It is not terribly old. A little over five hundred years. But the void it speaks of silently was and is from before the beginning. Older than any god or any creation. And it claims to be truer. All is illusory and has never been.

I came away chilled. I think of those who set out on the hippie trail in the sixties and did not come back. It never led here but it was often Buddhist in purpose. How many drug-wrecked mendicants or silent monks are left I have no idea. How alluring it was I remember. But a western mind reels at the thought of a world in which the existence of God is not even a question because nothing exists and only nothing. Few atheists deny their own being. Perhaps those who get beyond or behind all that are the truly blessed but Emma the cost. To know what it is to want to escape from personality one must know what personality is. Perhaps a void does underlie that dialectic. On Ryoanji's website there is a picture of the garden in snow. It seems no colder.

# XXXIX

It was a Friday. I was ill in bed in Detroit. I was not in my
usual room but in one much closer to the top of the stairs. I
guess so my mother could hear me should I call. The land-
ing was varnished pine along which I would fire my baby
howitzer against invisible foes. I think I must have been
drowsing when my mother came up to say The President
has been shot.

I lay and thought. This was something big. She came up
again not a great deal later to say The President has died.

On the Monday I went back to school able to report that
Jack Ruby formerly Jack Rubenstein had murdered the
alleged assassin Lee Harvey Oswald within the Dallas police
station. I had been reading newspapers since I was four but
news had never seemed so close or pressing.

From those days I have been an ardent careful watcher
of what happens in the voting-booths the churches the cau-
cuses the universities and the great debating-chambers of
the Republic. In the rather small mansion on Pennsylvania
Avenue with its tall receiving-rooms we visited as tourists
when President Kennedy must still have been working in the
West Wing. I'm reasonably good on the past and present of
the groupuscules of the French Left but hear me on the pre-
sent Governor of Kansas. This Emma you knew about me.

I was fluffing a sound-check at the new diminished
premises of the Poetry Society in Covent Garden. D turned
to W and said Of course there was more than one gunman.
I needed those words alone to be far into explaining loudly
why this might be wrong when I saw they were laughing.
You would have laughed like them but like them not
unkindly.

In one of the rooms of the house we rented there was a relief map of the United States. I can still feel the Alleghenies. Yearn for the big skies of Montana. I remember watching in a motel room reports of the trial of the killer of Medgar Evers but somehow I do not remember Dr King. Not then. From five years later. When the riots in Detroit came within blocks of the house we had rented five years earlier. A stoop. White clapboard. In the backyard the first evening the grey squirrels I had never seen before.

# XL

The only television I watched as an undergraduate was the
separate inaugural speech President Carter had recorded for
Europe on the subject of nuclear weapons. We just didn't.
Nowadays people have sets in their rooms. And mobiles.
They stay in touch with home friends and school friends in a
way impossible and unimaginable for us. They text and email.
This may be an epistemic shift but they feel terror loneliness
and grief no less than we did. I hear a boy sobbing behind a
breakwater phoning home. Telling passers-by he's OK.

# XLI

We are offered the Trinity as a model because we are ourselves trinities. To say God consists of three persons is to misunderstand. Say rather God makes himself manifest in three different ways but he is fully present in each of them at the moment of his manifestation.

Body resents the impositions of mind and expresses itself by for instance breaking wind in lifts or erupting with eczema.

Mind feels trapped in body. I look at my hand on the kitchen table an assemblage of skin flesh and as I age increasingly noticeable blood-vessels. When I die it will lie cold in the rigour of death.

The two fear and hate each other. The ribcage is a cage.

What binds them together is soul. In what theologians call perichoresis or circumincession they dance embracing. Body embraces mind and soul. Mind embraces soul and body. Soul embraces body and mind. Because mind and body are both fallible and belong to a fallen world they fail. Soul embracing them both goes on. I believe in the resurrection of the body. Soul and body without mind make no sense.

Emma whether I shall ever again see you face to face I do not know.

I know nothing beyond our horizon but biology cannot account for melody. Not in us. We are not birds or whales.

This does not and cannot abate my longing for you still to be in this world.

Emma.

Emma Smith.

# XLII

Only recently do I discover that at some point I ceased to think of my own death every night. I did so for at least ten years. Perhaps I'm worn out. Perhaps I have assimilated it.

There is so much I haven't told you. Blonde I in her white fake-fur jacket with ankles that were legend. J with her promising abundance. To whose wedding I went. Yes still. The lyric poet. The legion of my unattained.

W who has been my underpinning. Whom you would have enjoyed. Who would have made you laugh and think. Think and laugh.

# XLIII

S and I spent a day with D touring Elgar country. D was
preparing his radio play about the composer. One of the
country houses where Elgar was received in his fame was
Witley Court. The day hovered on the edge of rain when we
went there. Grey equal light. The air was very still. There
was no charge for admission. Two English Heritage workmen
were doing something in the orangery. The spectacular mid-
nineteenth-century house is a cavernous shell because of a
fire in 1937. We peeped in through empty casements and
saw photographs of the Prince of Wales early in the century
come here to shoot. We looked into Great Witley Church.
Its interior was brought from the Duke of Chandos' chapel
at Cannons. A baroque gem adrift in the green undulations
of Worcestershire. We walked on the south parterre. At one
corner a vast dry fountain. The largest outside Rome D
believed. Beyond it further lawn then ploughland. Ghosts of
Edwardian swagger. Empire assumed. Weekend parties. The
shooting and the dancing. Fifty household servants. More
your forebears' world than mine. When S and D and I visited
it would not yet have had the websites it has now. I take a
virtual tour of the church. I scroll sideways to take in the
panorama of the whole house. Steps columns balustrades.
Sky visible through window after window. It is hard to imag-
ine that it will ever be restored but it will not be let further
decay. Notices from the Department of the Environment.
English Heritage. You were English in that understated way
which makes no assertions about identity. I see a gazebo.
Long dresses.

# XLIV

Recently when I have gone to London I have seemed to see my younger self ahead of me. His darker hair and thinner face. His urgency as he travelled from editor to editor in the days when newspapers were still published from central London. The buzz he felt. Seeing his publishers. His rummaging in the Tottenham Court Road bookshops for American poetry. Then the dawn of the CD and the Virgin Megastore. Then the electronics shops. He was excited by the world as it moved on. He was part of what was happening.

He attends a literary committee meeting in a semi-basement room in Westminster. He and a friend come away and walk together down Whitehall. He imagines they look like two rising civil servants to the tourists. His friend praises the lines of the London Eye. Two civil servants. A poet and a major gay novelist.

I am what the poet was going to become. I have neither lived nor worked in London. As the city has grown more prosperous it has grown more careless. There are more beggars and the streets seem dirtier. As it clinks its jewellery and climbs into black cabs the city has become a stranger. A foreign country. Thanks to the Internet there is no real need to shop here any more. For some years the Evening Standard was sold where I live. Reading it felt like eavesdropping on a wider life. It stopped arriving and I soon stopped missing it. Now I don't always bother to buy it in London.

He dives into the Tube with brimming purpose. And you are dead.

## XLV

The English Faculty building in Oxford is modern and dull.
We were about to cross the road. I took the first step towards
a traffic island without looking properly. You screamed and I
jumped back as a car passed. You then gave me a cold and
furious telling-off. I suppose you had been shocked. At the
time it seemed unnecessarily drawn out. You were vivid and
magnificent.

It was something to learn that you could be so shocked.

I remember your high colouring on that cold day.

# XLVI

It was also in our first year that we attended a course of
lectures together. They were on modern poetry and they were
fascinating. We would talk afterwards and I would explain
why my emphases would have been different. I had read
more than you although I suspect you knew novels better.
Come Eighth Week the last week of term we arrived and sat
down beside each other as usual. Nobody appeared. We
realised that we were the only ones to stay the course. We
agreed to leave. We were sitting in a high row near the back.
As we left I glanced back and saw the lecturer making his
entrance in his black gown. I felt ashamed but there was no
turning back. We went to the Queen's Lane Coffee House.
You drank coffee. I also but I don't now remember whether it
was one of the rare celebratory times I allowed myself rhum
baba. Theirs was particularly inviting. So soaked in sugar-
syrup and rum that it gleamed. We were unusually at ease
with each other. Complicit.

# XLVII

S and I were invited down to Gloucestershire by a friend you
were staying with. We had lunch in his parents' cottage. You
admitted resenting your Second. You had never I knew enter-
tained dreams of an academic career. I am still not surprised.
You were a natural First. I noticed two pairs of slippers under
one bed but this was never alluded to. Neither of you gave
any indications of affection. We talked with winy freedom
otherwise. After lunch we went for a walk through the
woods. I remember you scuffing downhill through fallen
leaves and being as lost in enjoying it as any of us. The trees
were tall. There was the feeling of being in a large room and
the four of us having it to ourselves. I don't know how your
childhood divided between the house in Smith Square I never
saw and the country house I have also never seen. There was
pastoral in you. But you had also an urban sophistication.
You had the way of knowing how things happen I never
mastered. I was certain the man was not right for you. Day-
light stood in columns about us. I felt you were aching to
normalise yourself the one temptation to which you must
never yield. Not with all there was in you. Yet there was an
ordinary easy happiness about the day I remember from no
other time with you.

# XLVIII

You are an open wound in me. You were one of the most re-
markable people I have ever known. People who come across
members of your family hear of you and are curious to know
more though a generation has passed and you left so little
trace in the world. So small a footprint yet the shovelling
jealous sea has not erased it.

You were for me the necessary exemplary figure of dedi-
cation and endurance. Whatever your inner life truly was it
was ardently pursued. You observed with acute imagination.
When you spoke you drove at the heart of things though
sometimes through wry indirection. You manifested the value
of the life dedicated to an art. Whatever terrors you under-
went and they may have been very great you did not evince
them. You were never indecent.

Of course in making this thing about you or around you
I am talking about my youth and homesick for it. But that
is not the point. The point is that at one time in one place I
met someone who became to me a living conscience. Neither
parent nor role-model but a figure of the ideal. It was not my
imagination working but the meeting of two imaginations.
Our twinned vocations and ambitions. Our rivalries with
each other and with ourselves. As a courtly lover Troilus
becomes a better person because of his love for Criseyde. It
was like that but without desire. Oh lucky poet.

You have been with me all this time. It is getting late. This
afternoon the light settled in big shapeless areas of a weird
homeless yellow. I looked again and it was grey. It has now
slipped into blackness.

I think I must have repressed many memories of you.
Perhaps I feared you would out-power me. Perhaps after all

I was in love with you. I think not. Having no sister I didn't know how a brother–sister relationship worked. I didn't easily know how to be around girls. Mooncalf. I did love you but very rarely imagined you as a lover. Perhaps I wanted you trapped in virginity. If not mine then nobody's. Perhaps. I don't know how many baffles the mind can raise to conceal the source of the voice that is truly speaking. Life has not been as it would have been had you lived. Inevitably. But the only repressive agent I know of as powerful as whatever has withheld so much is guilt.

# XLIX

The events of the last few months or weeks of your life are
too scrambled to be sure of anything. There was Gloucester-
shire. I have a feeling you were among a party with S and D
and others at Joe Allen's in the then new new Covent Garden.
I must tentatively have invited you to stay. You came. We
walked. I can still see you kicking your way through fallen
leaves at the point where Kingsgate Road curves right to
meet St Cross Road. We were on the outside of the curve.
What must have happened is that you brought the poems
with you. I was being published as a reviewer though scarcely
yet as a poet. I was embarrassed that you of all people should
seek my advice.

# L

The poems. It is some years since I went to my grey filing-cabinet and took out the folder labelled Friends' MSS. A rusty paperclip gathers a postcard a letter and five poems. I shall make a new folder labelled Emma Smith to go to St Anne's your old college when I die. The postcard proposes the weekend of 23/24 October 1982. That can't have worked out because the thank-you letter was written on 4 November. It must have been 30/31 October that you came. You praise some of my poems. You refer to yours but I don't seem to have read them yet.

I have your last address again. In Fulham.

I have taken these papers into the kitchen for a better light. The poems are typed on flimsy paper. What I thought then I think now. They are astonishingly promising but not quite publishable. They are honest about abjection. They describe a failed love-affair. One of them has my name at the top but it is crossed out. You must have been selecting and not thinking. You have learnt something from Edith Sitwell about jingle. You have a capacious eye for detail. You do not have the whole personality which sings in your letter. How funny you were. How you could offer generalisations as experienced truth. It is clear that I was utterly miserable in my job. You are kind. There is no suggestion that we were ever anything other than friends.

You promise to send me your work in prose. The novel which had lain unmentionably beneath your bed must at last have been mentioned. I am astonished by your openness and by your wishing to be shot of the damned thing. Or not. One sickens of the sound of one's own voice. But you did not send it.

You died. I almost want to write you died instead.

# LI

This should have ended in Antarctica. Amid the sheeting whiteness your death would have been a symbolic closure. When Arthur Gordon Pym's narrative runs out he appears to be about to enter a hollow earth. To find something which has always underlain everything. And the Great Whale was white. Ahab dies pursuing the inscrutable. White has been a colour of joy and a colour of despair. Containing all colours it is none. A human form is seen against the white or enveloped in a rising blizzard. There may be an ambiguous gesture. To what the vanishing figure goes we shall never know. The human is overwhelmed by the larger and older mystery of impersonal nature. Gulls scream in the blistering wind. But it did not end there.

You fell off Lundy.

# LII

Lundy is an island twelve miles off the coast of North Devon. It was in the past noted for puffins but their number was already declining when you died. It is below nine hundred acres in area. Its human population excluding tourists is measured in double figures. Since 1969 it has been managed by the Landmark Trust. This was one of your father's concerns. It is believed that initially he spent £80,000 of his own money a year to do things like lay on electricity and gas restore the drains and import the materials needed for new building. I gawp. We were in our teens. Impossible to believe you never went there.

I am told that the grass sticks out at the edges of Lundy. That it is easy to take a step too far. I was told this at the time.

At the time I wondered what on earth you were doing there. Perhaps Antarctica had woken in you a passion for forsaken places. I knew nothing about your father.

Perhaps you inherited such a passion from him. Or perhaps you followed him to the ends of the earth to discover him. Or perhaps your dying there was an act of retribution. Or perhaps you were simply lost. A cuckoo in the family. I do not know. Neither do I know what the coroner found but the verdict must have been accidental death or open for not one of your father's obituaries refers to your suicide. Drifting girl you may have been one of those who cannot find a place for themselves in the world. Or you may have despaired of your own powers. In tears over your letter and poems I do not find one word one nuance that you wanted my help. And yet and yet. You came to me. You sought me out and then you died. I shall never in this life know whether or how I failed you. You.

# LIII

Maybe this has been a story of fathers all along. Of my father who had such leonine magnificence at the moment of his death. Whose last intelligible utterance had been a groan when my mother had briefly left the room. Of your father the slightly wayward public man. And a story of children. For we were scarcely more than that. And as children find one another in crowded places we did for a time find each other. In loving friendship. I am a father now. My two daughters and my son were born when you were already dead. If your novel survived you your family have it or it was thrown away unrecognised. There may be other poems blowing about the world.

Your father is said to have been highly observant funny sardonic and passionate for justice. You were like that.

When I was a child of about ten I was taken by friends on holiday to Bude in Cornwall. Their son was my friend and we fell out. Playing alone I met a girl of my own age. An only child. We played together for a couple of days. I explained I would be going home the next day. At our last meeting she produced a trinket of some sort I think a plastic ring. We were standing on a sandy path a little way above the beach. She asked me to keep it to remember her by. Obscurely embarrassed by knowing the gift must be a loss for her I replied grandiloquently that I remembered what I wanted to remember and did not need a souvenir.

I have remembered her.

I have remembered you.

## LIV

*Envoi*

So little my book go tell them all.

Oh Emma.